Twenty Prose Poems

❧ ❧

Charles Baudelaire

Translated by
Michael Hamburger

City Lights Books
San Francisco

Translated from the French *Petits Poèmes en Prose*

Published in England
by Jonathan Cape Ltd, 1968

© 1946, 1968, 1988 by Michael Hamburger

First City Lights Books edition 1988

Designed by Patricia Fujii
Typesetting by Re/Search

Library of Congress Cataloging-in-Publication Data

Baudelaire, Charles, 1821-1867.
    Twenty prose poems.

    French text and English translation of: Petits
poèmes en prose.
      I. Hamburger, Michael. II. Title.
PQ2191.P4E5 1988   841'.8   88-1047
ISBN 0-87286-216-X

City Lights Books are available to bookstores through our primary distributor:
Subterranean Company. P. O. Box 168, 265 S. 5th St., Monroe, OR 97456.
503-847-5274. Toll-free orders 800-274-7826. FAX 503-847-6018. Our books are
also available through library jobbers and regional distributors.
For personal orders and catalogs, please write to City Lights Books, 261 Columbus
Avenue, San Francisco CA 94133.

CITY LIGHTS BOOKS are edited by Lawrence Ferlinghetti and Nancy J. Peters
and published at the City Lights Bookstore, 261 Columbus Avenue, San Francisco,
CA 94133.

TABLE OF CONTENTS

INTRODUCTION

❧ BAUDELAIRE'S PROSE poems, or *Little Poems in Prose*, were written at long intervals during the last twelve or thirteen years of his life. Most of them were published separately in periodicals, but the complete set of fifty prose poems was not published until 1869, two years after Baudelaire's death. He had at one time planned to write a hunded of them, but his singular lack of energy and of facility always stood between his plans and their realization. In the prose poem *"Les Projets"* Baudelaire summed up that characteristic distrust of action which affected even his literary output: 'Why force my body to change its place, when my soul travels so lightly and so swiftly? And what is the good of carrying out a project, when the project itself gives me pleasure enough?'

Although Baudelaire was perfectly capable of writing longer prose works, like *Les Paradis artificiels* or the critical essays collected in *L'Art romantique*, the prose poem was a medium much better suited to his habits and character. Being pre-eminently a moralist, he needed a medium that enabled him to illustrate a moral insight as briefly and as vividly as possible. Being an artist and a sensualist, he needed a medium that was not epigrammatic or aphoristic, but allowed him scope for fantasy and for that element of vagueness or suggestiveness which he considered essential to beauty. As a moralist, Baudelaire can be seen as a late representative of the French classical tradition. As an artist and aesthetician, he drew on Romanticism and prepared the way for Symbolism, which has come to be regarded as a development of Romanticism. The prose poem satisified both requirements: it could make a point, without too much argument or elaboration, and it could render a poetic state of mind in images akin to those in Baudelaire's verse. Above all, it was short — an inestima-

1

ble advantage to a writer who subscribed to Poe's theory of the short poem, who had never liked regular or sustained work and who in later years, as his letters show, became almost obsessed with *le vide papier que la blancheur défend.*

Unlike the *Fleurs du mal,* the *Petits Poèmes en prose* were not intended to be read as a sequence. In Baudelaire's own words the work 'has neither head nor tail since, on the contrary, everything in it is both head and tail at the same time, alternately and reciprocally.'* Some of the prose poems — *"L'Invitation au voyage"* is a striking instance — are the complement in prose of poems in *Les Fleurs du mal.* Others, such as *"Le Joueur généreux"* or *"Assommons les pauvres,"* develop themes barely intimated in the book of poems, though clearly stated in Baudelaire's notebooks, *Mon Cœur mis à nu* and *Fusées.* Yet in either case the theme is less crucial than the medium. A comparison of the prose poem *"Invitation to the Voyage"* with the lyrical poem "Invitation au voyage" is instructive for that very reason : the title and the theme are the same, but nothing that the prose poem says can match the effect of

> Mon enfant, ma sœur,
> Songe à la douceur . . .

A great deal has been written about the probable sources of the medium used by Baudelaire; but such works as Maurice de Guerin's *Le Centaure* or even Aloysius Bertrand's *Gaspard de la nuit* have little in common with Baudelaire's prose poems. In his letter to Houssaye which usually serves as a preface to the prose poems, Baudelaire mentioned that *Gaspard de la nuit* had inspired him with the wish to write a book of the same type, but he also admitted that the finished work differed greatly from his models. As for the influence of Houssaye himself, of which Baudelaire also speaks, we can dismiss this as a compliment to a friend. If the literary ancestry of Baudelaire's prose poems must be established, Edgar Allan Poe and De Quincey, rather than the initiators of the French prose poem as such, have the most substantial claim, if only because Baudelaire had familiarized himself with their work to a degree which only translation permits.

2

I have called the prose poem a medium because it is not a form. The special importance of the prose poem in nineteenth-century French literature has to do with the limitations of French verse. Before the establishment of *vers libre* as a recognized medium for poetry it was the prose poem alone that gave French poets a kind of freedom which English poets had enjoyed for centuries. In a literature that had never evolved a medium as flexible as Shakespeare's blank verse, the only alternative to strict metre and rhyme was prose. Victor Hugo's metrical innovations did not decisively alter this situation; and Baudelaire's prosody in *Les Fleurs du mal* owed little to Victor Hugo's reforms. In *Les Fleurs du mal*, therefore, Baudelaire's modernity had to assert itself in the teeth of classical metres and a classical rhetoric. If it has become difficult for us to appreciate the originality of Baudelaire's poetry, the conventions of French prosody, and especially its rhetoric, are to blame. Rimbaud, a more extreme reformer and innovator in that regard, was one of the earliest of Baudelaire's readers to imply as much in the reservations added to his description of Baudelaire as *'le premier voyant, roi des poètes.'* This is not to suggest for a moment that Baudelaire's prose poems are superior to the verse of *Les Fleurs du mal*; but they are different, and they are more translatable, at least as far as Baudelaire the moralist is concerned; and it could be that Baudelaire's moral acumen and courage have more to say to us at present than his cult of delicate and exquisite sensations.

Even in the prose poems Baudelaire indulges in a vocabulary which English readers have come to associate with the aestheticism of the eighteen nineties. No other literary convention that I can think of has become so remote and unacceptable in so short a time. It is as well to admit that the atrocities of our century have hardened us against the shock effects on which Baudelaire's vocabulary once relied. The 'enormities' of his Epilogue to the *Prose Poems* — brothels, bandits, convict hulks, and the 'infernal charms' of an aged whore — are now unlikely to give us that 'new shudder' which Baudelaire's comfortably bourgeois readers may well have experienced when confronted with so drastic a diagnosis

of their own civilization — or 'syphilization,' as Baudelaire once preferred to call it. Baudelaire had no choice but to draw on the 'enormities' of his own time. Those of us who fail to see that his vision and insight go much deeper than the paraphernalia of Parisian vice — to 'a sickness unto death' that is still ours, though its symptoms have changed — will share the impatience of Henry James, an impatience 'of the same order as that which we should feel if a poet, pretending to pluck the *Flowers of Good*, should come and present us, as specimens, a rhapsody on plumcake and *eau de Cologne*.'*

If Baudelaire had been no more than a mid-nineteenth-century Parisian dandy perversely aware of the seamy side of the city which he loved and celebrated, aware of the bad smells, the poverty and the prostitution, he might still be a considerable poet, since no such awareness bothered the purveyors of poetic *eau de Cologne* to a class that did well out of the bad smells, the poverty and the prostitution; but even Baudelaire's detractors, such as Sartre, acknowledge that he was a great deal more than that. Baudelaire's 'subjectivity' and apparent egocentricity are misleading. Poets and moralists, unlike biologists, are not provided with guinea pigs and white rats on which they can test their theories; they must content themselves with a limited measure of insight into the minds and motives of others, and the rather more reliable evidence of self-knowledge. Certainly we must allow for a certain amount of inconsistency, if not of self-contradiction, in the moral substance of Baudelaire's work. Baudelaire was his own guinea pig; and in his experiments he made ample use of masks, of what Yeats called the 'anti-self' or 'antithetical self.' Whether in the first person singular or not, many of Baudelaire's statements are experimental in this way, not to say dialectical. Yet it was for the sake of an impersonal truth that he sacrificed his personal vanity and dignity, to the extent of confessing to crimes which he had never committed. His only recompense — and that a small one — for the sacrifice was the pleasure to be derived from shocking a complacent public by an open exhibition of its secret indecencies. This too was his bond — perhaps his only bond — with his brother, the 'hypocritical reader.'

4

Baudelaire, of course, could not foresee all the kinds of analysis for which he provided the data, from the Freudian psycho-analysis of René Laforgue to the existential psycho-analysis of Jean-Paul Sartre and the psycho-criticism of Charles Mauron; but his sacrifice had insured him in advance against every kind of judgment, contemporary or posthumous. 'To be, *above all else, a great man* and a *saint* in one's own eyes,' he wrote in his journals, omitting to italicize the operative words — 'in one's own eyes.' What is more, Baudelaire did his best not to be a great man or a saint in anybody else's eyes : 'When I have inspired universal horror and disgust,' he also wrote, 'I shall have conquered solitude.' Yet even Sartre, who used Baudelaire's case to demonstrate how men choose their own hell, ended by recognizing 'Baudelaire's nobility and greatness as a man,' because 'flabbiness, abandonment and slackness seemed to Baudelaire unforgivable sins.'

It was Baudelaire — in the introductory poem to *Les Fleurs du mal* — who classed boredom among the deadly sins, and this alone assures him a place among the great moralists and psychologists. Here again he profited by laying bare his own heart with a rigour which most of the classical moralists applied only to the conduct of others. Sartre is right when he suggests:

> If we could put out of our minds the exaggerated vocabulary which Baudelaire used to describe himself, forget words like 'frightful,' 'nightmare' and 'horror,' which occur on every page of *Les Fleurs du mal*, and penetrate right into his heart, we should perhaps find beneath the anguish, the remorse and the vibrating nerves something gentler and much more intolerable than the most painful of ills — Indifference.

But Baudelaire himself said more than that in the introductory poem, when he speaks of Boredom 'that would gladly reduce the earth to rubble and swallow the world in a great yawn.' It was out of his experience of this Boredom that Baudelaire constructed his dualism of *'spleen'* and *'idéal,'* his knowledge of what he called the 'abyss' and our need to escape from it

5

perpetually by creating illusions and ideals of one kind or another.

Baudelaire's modernity, then, must be looked for not in his 'exaggerated vocabulary' but in a capacity for facing the naked truth which he shared with men like Leopardi, Kierkegaard and Nietzsche. In spite of all that has been written about him — or even because of it — Baudelaire's theological position remains a conundrum, and it is best to leave it alone here. Catholics have seen him as a Catholic, puritans as a puritan — or 'puritan inside out,' as Aldous Huxley called him —atheists as an atheist, existentialists as an existentialist, and so forth. Baudelaire was deeply impressed by the writings of Pascal, but even the Jansenist influence does not account for his peculiar attitude to questions of good and evil — an attitude which at one time earned him the title of 'Satanist.' Certain Calvinist doctrines are suggested by Baudelaire's conviction that 'wickedness is always inexcusable, but there is some merit in knowing that one is wicked; and the most irreparable of vices is to do evil without knowing it.' This is how he puts it in the prose poem *La Fausse Monnaie*. In his poem *L'Irrémédiable* he speaks of

> Soulagement et gloire uniques,
> — La Conscience dans le Mal.

John Henry Newman defined the moral doctrine of the Calvinists as follows:

But they go on to say, as I understand them, very differently from Catholicism, that the converted and the unconverted can be discriminated by man, that the justified are conscious of their state of justification, and that the regenerate cannot fall away. Catholics, on the other hand, shade and soften the awful antagonism between good and evil, which is one of their dogmas, by holding that there are different degrees of justification, that there is a great difference in point of gravity between sin and sin, that there is the possibility and danger of falling

away, and that there is no certain knowledge given to any one that he is simply in a state of grace, and much less that he is to persevere to the end.

What is certain about Baudelaire is that he did not attempt to 'shade and soften the awful antagonism between good and evil,' but sharpened it by relegating good to the realm of the ideal; and his insistence on being 'a saint in his own eyes' is difficult to reconcile with any form of Christian orthodoxy, though he did define progress as 'the diminution of the traces of original sin.' The same contradictions and complexities attach to Baudelaire's political opinions. Like other French writers of his time — Flaubert, Leconte de Lisle and the brothers Goncourt, for instance — he detested the 'progressive' cant of the newspapers and politicians. On the one hand he was capable of an aphorsim like this one: 'If a poet demanded from the State the right to keep a bourgeois in his stable, people would be very much astonished, but if a bourgeois asked for some roast poet, people would think it quite natural.' This, of course, was a squib, from Baudelaire's notebook called *Fusées*; and something of the same desire to shock is apparent in his prose poem *"Let's Beat up the Poor,"* though it makes a perfectly serious and original point about the inadequacy of mere benevolence and compassion. On the other hand, Baudelaire felt a compassion with the poor, the exploited and the sick that is amply attested in all his works, including many which do not resort to such extreme and revolutionary solutions. His thinking about society and politics, as about everything else, was experimental; like the thinking of most poets, it drew on experience and imagination, rather than on facts and general arguments. That is another reason why the prose poem proved a medium so congenial to Baudelaire.

M.H.
Lerwick, 1944
London, 1967

*Dedicatory Letter to Arsène Houssaye.

*Henry James, *French Poets and Novelists* (London 1884), p. 62.

Twenty Prose Poems

I

LE DÉSESPOIR DE LA VIEILLE

❧ LA PETITE vieille ratatinée se sentit toute réjouie en voyant ce joli enfant à qui chacun faisait fête, à qui tout le monde voulait plaire; ce joli être, si fragile comme elle, la petite vieille, et, comme elle aussi, sans dents et sans cheveux.

Et elle s'approcha de lui, voulant lui faire des risettes et des mines agréables.

Mais l'enfant épouvanté se débattait sous les caresses de la bonne femme décrépite, et remplissait la maison de ses glapissements.

Alors la bonne vieille se retira dans sa solitude éternelle, et elle pleurait dans un coin, se disant : — « Ah! pour nous, malheureuses vieilles femelles, l'âge est passé de plaire, même aux innocents; et nous faisons horreur aux petits enfants que nous voulons aimer! »

I

THE OLD WOMAN'S DESPAIR

❧ THE LITTLE, shrivelled old woman felt quite overjoyed when she saw the pretty child whom everyone wished to amuse, whom everyone tried to please; that pretty creature, so fragile, like herself, the little old woman, and, like her also, without teeth and without hair.

And she approached the child, wishing to smile at it and make faces pleasantly.

But the terrified child struggled against the caresses of the good, decrepit woman, and filled the house with its yelping.

Then the kind old woman retired into her eternal solitude, and cried in a corner, saying to herself : 'Oh! for us wretched old females, the age when we could please, if only the innocent, is past; and we fill with horror the little children whom we wish to love!'

II

LE *CONFITEOR* DE L'ARTISTE

❧ QUE LES fins de journées d'automne sont pénétrantes! Ah! pénétrantes jusqu'à la douleur! car il est de certaines sensations délicieuses dont le vague n'exclut pas l'intensité; et il n'est pas de pointe plus acérée que celle de l'Infini.

Grande délice que celui de noyer son regard dans l'immensité du ciel et de la mer! Solitude, silence, incomparable chasteté de l'azur! une petite voile frissonnante à l'horizon, et qui par sa petitesse et son isolement imite mon irrémédiable existence, mélodie monotone de la houle, toutes ces choses pensent par moi, ou je pense par elles (car dans la grandeur de la rêverie, le *moi* se perd vite!); elles pensent, dis-je, mais musicalement et pittoresquement, sans arguties, san syllogismes, sans déductions.

Toutefois, ces pensées, qu'elles sortent de moi ou s'élancent des choses, deviennent bientôt trop intenses. L'énergie dans la volupté crée un malaise et une souffrance positive. Mes nerfs trop tendus ne donnent plus que des vibrations criardes et douloureuses.

Et maintenant la profondeur du ciel me consterne; sa limpidité m'exaspère. L'insensibilité de la mer, l'immuabilité du spectacle me révoltent . . . Ah! faut-il éternellement souffrir, ou fuir éternellement le beau? Nature, enchanteresse sans pitié, rivale toujours victorieuse, laisse-moi! Cesse de tenter mes désirs et mon orgueil! L'étude du beau est un duel où l'artiste crie de frayeur avant d'être vaincu.

II

CONFITEOR OF THE ARTIST

❦ HOW PENETRATING are the ends of days in autumn! Oh! penetrating to the point of grief! For there are certain delicious sensations whose vagueness does not exclude intensity; and no point is sharper than that of the Infinite.

Oh, the vast delight of gazing fixedly, drowning one's glance in the immensity of sky and sea! Solitude, silence, incomparable chastity of the azure! A little sailing-boat shuddering on the horizon, the paradigm, in its littleness and its isolation, of my irretrievable existence; monotonous melody of the surge; all these things reflect my thoughts, or I reflect theirs (for in the grandeur of reverie the *ego* is soon lost); they think, as I say, but musically and picturesquely, without quibbling, without syllogism, without deduction.

Nevertheless, these thoughts, whether formed within me or projected from things, soon grow too intense. The energy which pleasure does not absorb creates a kind of unrest and a positive pain. My nerves, now excessively tense, transmit only wailing and sorrowful vibrations.

And now the profundity of the sky perplexes me; the limpid light exasperates me. The insensitiveness of the sea, the immobility of the scene, revolt me. Oh, must we suffer eternally, or flee eternally from all that is beautiful? Nature, unpitying enchantress, ever–victorious rival, let me be! Leave off tempting my desires and my pride! The study of beauty is a duel in which the artist cries out in terror before being vanquished.

III

LA CHAMBRE DOUBLE

᪥ UNE CHAMBRE qui ressemble à une rêverie, une chambre véritablement *spirituelle*, où l'atmosphère stagnante est légèrement teintée de rose et de bleu.

L'âme y prend un bain de paresse, aromatisé par le regret et le désir. — C'est quelque chose de crépusculaire, de bleuâtre et de rosâtre; un rêve de volupté pendant une éclipse.

Les meubles ont des formes allongées, prostrées, alanguies. Les meubles ont l'air de rêver; on les dirait doués d'une vie somnambulique, comme le végétal et le minéral. Les étoffes parlent une langue muette, comme les fleurs, comme les ciels, comme les soleils couchants.

Sur les murs nulle abomination artistique. Relativement au rêve pur, à l'impression non analysée, l'art défini, l'art positif est un blasphème. Ici, tout a la suffisante clarté et la délicieuse obscurité de l'harmonie.

Une senteur infinitésimale du choix le plus exquis, à laquelle se mêle une trés-légère humidité, nage dans cette atmosphère, où l'esprit sommeillant est bercé par des sensations de serre chaude.

La mousseline pleut abondamment devant les fenêtres et devant le lit; elle s'épanche en cascades neigeuses. Sur ce lit est couchée l'Idole, la souveraine des rêves. Mais comment est-elle ici? Qui l'a amenée? quel pouvoir magique l'a installée sur ce trône de rêverie et de volupté? Qu'importe? la voilà! je la reconnais.

Voilà bien ces yeux dont la flamme traverse le crépuscule; ces subtiles et terribles *mirettes*, que je reconnais à leur effrayante malice! Elles attirent, elles subjuguent, elles dévo-

14

III

THE DOUBLE ROOM

❧ A ROOM that is like a reverie, a room truly soulful, where the stagnant atmosphere is lightly tinted with rose-colour and blue.

There the soul bathes in idleness, made fragrant by regret and desire. It is a thing of twilight, bluish and roseate; a dream of delicious pleasures during an eclipse.

The furniture is formed of elongated, prostrated, languishing shapes. The furniture appears to be dreaming; it seems endowed with a somnambulistic life, like vegetables or minerals. The cloth materials speak a silent language, like flowers, like skies, like setting suns.

No artistic abomination on the walls. In relation to the pure dream, to the impression left unanalysed, definite art, positive art is a blasphemy. Here all things possess the required clarity and the delicious vagueness of harmony.

An infinitesimal odour most exquisitely chosen, which is mingled with a very slight dampness, floats in this atmosphere, where the soul in a trance is lulled by hot-house sensations.

Muslin flows abundantly from the windows and from the bed; it pours out in snowy cascades. On the bed lies the Idol, the sovereign of dreams. But how does she come to be here? What magic power has established her on this throne of reverie and voluptuous delights? What does it matter? She is here, and I recognize her!

These, indeed, are the eyes whose flame pierces the twilight; these are the subtle and terrible eyes which I recognize by their dreadful malice! They attract, they subjugate, they

rent le regard de l'imprudent qui les contemple. Je les ai souvent étudiées, ces étoiles noires qui commandent la curiosité et l'admiration.

A quel démon bienveillant dois-je d'être ainsi entouré de mystère, de silence, de paix et de parfums? O béatitude! ce que nous nommons généralement la vie, même dans son expansion la plus heureuse, n'a rien de commun avec cette vie suprême dont j'ai maintenant connaissance et que je savoure minute par minute, seconde par seconde!

Non! il n'est plus de minutes, il n'est plus de secondes! Le temps a disparu; c'est l'Éternité qui règne, une éternité de délices!

Mais un coup terrible, lourd, a retenti à la porte, et, comme dans les rêves infernaux, il m'a semblé que je recevais un coup de pioche dans l'estomac.

Et puis un Spectre est entré. C'est un huissier qui vient me torturer au nom de la loi; une infâme concubine qui vient crier misère et ajouter les trivialités de sa vie aux douleurs de la mienne; ou bien le saute-ruisseau d'un directeur de journal qui réclame la suite du manuscrit.

La chambre paradisiaque, l'idole, la souveraine des rêves, la *Sylphide*, comme disait le grand René, toute cette magie a disparu au coup brutal frappé par le Spectre.

Horreur! je me souviens! je me souviens! Oui! ce taudis, ce séjour de l'éternel ennui, est bien le mien. Voici les meubles sots, poudreux, écornés; la cheminée sans flamme et sans braise, souillée de crachats : les tristes fenêtres où la pluie a tracé des sillons dans la poussiére; les manuscrits, raturés ou incomplets; l'almanach où le crayon a marqué les dates sinistres!

Et ce parfum d'un autre monde, dont je m'enivrais avec une sensibilité perfectionnée, hélas! il est remplacé par une fétide odeur de tabac mêlée à je ne sais quelle nauséabonde moisissure. On respire ici maintenant le ranci de la désolation.

Dans ce monde étroit, mais si plein de dégoût, un seul objet connu me sourit : la fiole de laudanum; une vieille et terrible amie; comme toutes les amies, hélas! féconde en caresses et en traîtrises.

devour the gaze of the impudent man who contemplates them. I have often studied them, those black stars that call for both curiosity and admiration.

To what benevolent demon do I owe the joy of being thus surrounded with mystery, with silence, with peace and with perfumes? O beatitude! That which we generally call life, even when it is fullest and happiest, has nothing in common with that supreme life with which I am now acquainted and which I am tasting minute by minute, second by second!

No! there are no more minutes, there are no more seconds! Time has disappeared; it is Eternity that reigns now, an eternity of delights!

But on the door a terrible, heavy knock has resounded, and, as in some infernal dream, it seemed to me that my stomach received a blow struck by a pick-axe. And then a Spectre entered. It is a bailiff who has come to torture me in the name of the law; an infamous concubine who has come to proclaim misery and to add the trivialities of her life to the sorrows of mine; or else the errand-boy of the editor of some newspaper who is asking for the sequel to the manuscript.

The paradisiac room, the idol, the sovereign of dreams, the *Sylphide*, as the great René called her, all this magic has vanished with the brutal blow struck by the Spectre.

Oh Horror! I remember! I remember! Yes! this hovel, that dwelling-place of eternal boredom, is, after all, my own. Here is the stupid furniture, dirty, with chipped corners; the fireplace without flame and without embers, sullied by spittle, the dreary windows on which the rain has traced furrows in the dust; the manuscripts, effaced or incomplete; the almanac in which my pencil has marked sinister dates!

And that perfume of another world, with which I inebriated myself by means of a perfected sensibility, alas, is replaced by a fetid odour of tobacco mixed with some indescribably nauseating mustiness. Now the room is filled with the rancid air of desolation.

In this world so narrow and yet so full of disgust, only one familiar object invites me : the phial of laudanum; an old and terrible mistress, and, like all mistresses, liberal of caresses and betrayals.

Oh! oui! le Temps a reparu; le Temps règne en souverain maintenant; et avec le hideux vieillard est revenu tout son démoniaque cortège de Souvenirs, de Regrets, de Spasmes, de Peurs, d'Angoisses, de Cauchemars, de Colères et de Névroses.

Je vous assure que les secondes maintenant sont fortement et solennellement accentuées, et chacune, en jaillissant de la pendule, dit : — « Je suis la Vie, l'insupportable, l'implacable Vie! »

Il n'y a qu'une seconde dans la vie humaine qui ait mission d'annoncer une bonne nouvelle, la *bonne nouvelle* qui cause à chacun une inexplicable peur.

Oui! le Temps régne; il a repris sa brutale dictature. Et il me pousse, comme si j'étais un bœuf, avec son double aiguillon. — « Et hue donc! bourrique! Sue donc, esclave! Vis donc, damné! »

Oh yes, Time has returned; now Time reigns absolute; and with the hideous old man the whole of his demoniac retinue has returned, Memories, Regrets, Spasms, Fears, Afflictions, Nightmares, Rages and Neuroses.

I assure you that now the seconds are strongly and solemnly accentuated and each one, spouting out of the clock, says : 'I am Life, insupportable, implacable Life!'

There is only one second in the life of men whose mission it is to announce good news, the *good news* which fills every man with an inexplicable fear.

Yes! Time rules now; he has resumed his brutal dictatorship. He pushes me, as though I were an ox, with his two-pronged goad : 'Move on there, beast! Sweat, you slave! Live, convict, live!'

IV

LE FOU ET LA VÉNUS

🌿 QUELLE ADMIRABLE journée! Le vaste parc se pâme sous l'œil brûlant du soleil, comme la jeunesse sous la domination de l'Amour.

L'extase universelle des choses ne s'exprime par aucun bruit; les eaux elles-mêmes sont comme endormies. Bien différente des fêtes humaines, c'est ici une orgie silencieuse.

On dirait qu'une lumière toujours croissante fait de plus en plus étinceler les objets; que les fleurs excitées brûlent du désir de rivaliser avec l'azur du ciel par l'énergie de leurs couleurs, et que la chaleur, rendant visibles les parfums, les fait monter vers l'astre, comme des fumées.

Cependant, dans cette jouissance universelle, j'ai aperçu un être affligé.

Aux pieds d'une colossale Vénus, un de ces fous artificiels, un de ces bouffons volontaires chargés de faire rire les rois quand le Remords ou l'Ennui les obsède, affublé d'un costume éclatant et ridicule, coiffé de cornes et de sonnettes, tout ramassé contre le piédestal, lève des yeux pleins de larmes vers l'immortelle Déesse.

Et ses yeux disent : — « Je suis le dernier et le plus solitaire des humains, privé d'amour et d'amitié, et bien inférieur en cela au plus imparfait des animaux. Cependant je suis fait, moi aussi, pour comprendre et sentir l'immortelle Beauté! Ah! Déesse! ayez pitié de ma tristesse et de mon délire! »

Mais l'implacable Vénus regarde au loin je ne sais quoi avec ses yeux de marbre.

IV

THE FOOL AND THE VENUS

꽃 WHAT AN admirable day! The vast park abandons itself to the scorching eye of the sun, like youth to the domination of Love.

The universal ecstasy of created things does not express itself in any sound; the flowing streams, even, are as though asleep. Quite unlike human festivities, this is a silent orgy.

It seems as though an ever-growing radiance were making the objects sparkle more and more; as though the excited flowers were burning with the desire to rival the azure of the sky in the intensity of their colours, and that the heat, rendering all perfumes visible, were causing them to rise towards the luminary like flying fireworks.

However, amongst this universal rejoicing, I have discovered an afflicted creature.

At the feet of a colossal Venus, one of those artificial fools, one of those wilful clowns whose duty it is to make kings laugh when Remorse or Boredom obsesses them, dressed up in a garish and ridiculous costume, crowned with cap and bells, huddled up close to the pedestal, raises his eyes filled with tears to the immortal Goddess.

And his eyes say : 'I am the lowest and most solitary of men, deprived of love and friendship, and, in this respect, greatly inferior to the most imperfect of animals. Yet I, even I, was made to understand and feel immortal Beauty! O Goddess, have pity on my sadness and on my frenzy!'

But the implacable Venus gazes far into the distance at some object or other with her marble eyes.

V

A UNE HEURE DU MATIN

≪ ENFIN! SEUL! On n'entend plus que le roulement de quelques fiacres attardés et éreintés. Pendant quelques heures, nous posséderons le silence, sinon le repos. Enfin! la tyrannie de la face humaine a disparu, et je ne souffrirai plus que par moi-même.

Enfin! il m'est donc permis de me délasser dans un bain de ténèbres! D'abord, un double tour à la serrure. Il me semble que ce tour de clef augmentera ma solitude et fortifiera les barricades qui me séparent actuellement du monde.

Horrible vie! Horrible ville! Récapitulons la journée : avoir vu plusieurs hommes de lettres, dont l'un m'a demandé si l'on pouvait aller en Russie par voie de terre (il prenait sans doute la Russie pour une île); avoir disputé généreusement contre le directeur d'une revue, qui à chaque objection répondait : « — C'est ici le parti des honnêtes gens », ce qui implique que tous les autres journaux sont rédigés par des coquins; avoir salué une vingtaine de personnes, dont quinze me sont inconnues; avoir distribué des poignées de main dans la même proportion, et cela sans avoir pris la précaution d'acheter des gants; être monté pour tuer le temps, pendant une averse, chez une sauteuse qui m'a prié de lui dessiner un costume de *Vénustre*; avoir fait ma cour à un directeur de théâtre, qui m'a dit en me congédiant : « — Vous feriez peut-être bien de vous adresser à Z . . .; c'est le plus lourd, le plus sot et le plus célèbre de tous mes auteurs; avec lui vous pourriez peut-être aboutir à quelque chose. Voyez-le, et puis nous verrons »; m'être vanté (pourquoi?) de plusieurs vilaines actions que je n'ai jamais commises, et avoir lâchement nié quelques autres méfaits que j'ai accomplis avec joie, délit de fanfaronnade,

AT ONE O'CLOCK IN THE MORNING

❦ ALONE, AT last! Not a sound to be heard but the rumbling of some belated and decrepit cabs. For a few hours we shall have silence, if not repose. At last the tyranny of the human face has disappeared, and I myself shall be the only cause of my sufferings.

At last, then, I am allowed to refresh myself in a bath of darkness! First of all, a double turn of the lock. It seems to me that this twist of the key will increase my solitude and fortify he barricades which at this instant separate me from the world.

Horrible life! Horrible town! Let us recapitulate the day : seen several men of letters, one of whom asked me whether one could go to Russia by a land route (no doubt he took Russia to be an island); disputed generously with the editor of a review, who, to each of my objections, replied : 'We represent the cause of decent people,' which implies that all the other newspapers are edited by scoundrels; greeted some twenty persons, with fifteen of whom I am not acquainted; distributed handshakes in the same proportion, and this without having taken the precaution of buying gloves; to kill time, during a shower, went to see an acrobat, who asked me to design for her the costume of a *Venustra*; paid court to the director of a theatre, who, while dismissing me, said to me : 'Perhaps you would do well to apply to Z——; he is the clumsiest, the stupidest and the most celebrated of my authors; together with him, perhaps, you would get somewhere. Go to see him, and after that we'll see;' boasted (why?) of several vile actions which I have never committed, and faint-heartedly denied some other misdeeds which I accomplished

crime de respect humain; avoir refusé à un ami un service facile, et donné une recommandation écrite à un parfait drôle; ouf! est-ce bien fini?

Mécontent de tous et mécontent de moi, je voudrais bien me racheter et m'enorgueillir un peu dans le silence et la solitude de la nuit. Ames de ceux que j'ai aimés, âmes de ceux que j'ai chantés, fortifiez-moi, soutenez-moi, éloignez de moi le mensonge et les vapeurs corruptrices du monde; et vous, Seigneur mon Dieu! accordez-moi la grâce de produire quelques beaux vers qui me prouvent à moi-même que je ne suis pas le dernier des hommes, que je ne suis pas inférieur à ceux que je méprise!

with joy, an error of bravado, an offence against human respect; refused a friend an easy service, and gave a written recommendation to a perfect clown; oh, isn't that enough?

Discontented with everyone and discontented with myself, I would gladly redeem myself and elate myself a little in the silence and solitude of night. Souls of those I have loved, souls of those I have sung, strengthen me, support me, rid me of lies and the corrupting vapours of the world; and you, O Lord God, grant me the grace to produce a few good verses, which shall prove to myself that I am not the lowest of men, that I am not inferior to those whom I despise.

VI

LES FOULES

❧ IL N'EST pas donné à chacun de prendre un bain de multitude : jouir de la foule est un art; et celui-là seul peut faire, aux dépens du genre humain, une ribote de vitalité, à qui une fée a insufflé dans son berceau le goût du travestissement et du masque, la haine du domicile et la passion du voyage.

Multitude, solitude : termes égaux et convertibles pour le poëte actif et fécond. Qui ne sait pas peupler sa solitude, ne sait pas non plus être seul dans une foule affairée.

Le poëte jouit de cet incomparable privilège, qu'il peut à sa guise être lui-même et autrui. Comme ces âmes errantes qui cherchent un corps, il entre, quand il veut, dans le personnage de chacun. Pour lui seul, tout est vacant; et si de certaines places paraissent lui être fermées, c'est qu'à ses yeux elles ne valent pas la peine d'être visitées.

Le promeneur solitaire et pensif tire une singulière ivresse de cette universelle communion. Celui-là qui épouse facilement la foule connaît des jouissances fiévreuses, dont seront éternellement privés l'égoïste, fermé comme un coffre, et le paresseux, interné comme un mollusque. Il adopte comme siennes toutes les professions, toutes les joies et toutes les misères que la circonstance lui présente.

Ce que les hommes nomment amour est bien petit, bien restreint et bien faible, comparé à cette ineffable orgie, à cette sainte prostitution de l'âme qui se donne tout entière, poésie et charité, à l'imprévu qui se montre, à l'inconnu qui passe.

Il est bon d'apprendre quelquefois aux heureux de ce monde, ne fût-ce pour humilier un instant leur sot orgueil, qu'il est des bonheurs supérieurs au leur, plus vastes et plus

VI

CROWDS

❧ IT IS not given to everyone to take a bath in the multitude; to enjoy the crowd is an art; and only that man can gorge himself with vitality, at the expense of the human race, whom, in his cradle, a fairy has inspired with love of disguise and of the mask, with hatred of the home and a passion for voyaging.

Multitude, solitude : terms that, to the active and fruitful poet, are synonymous and interchangeable. A man who cannot people his solitude is no less incapable of being alone in a busy crowd.

The poet enjoys the incomparable privilege that he can, at will, be either himself or another. Like those wandering spirits that seek a body, he enters, when he likes, into the person of any man. For him alone all is vacant; and if certain places seem to be closed to him, it is that, to his eyes, they are not worth the trouble of being visited.

The solitary and pensive pedestrian derives a singular exhilaration from this universal communion. That man who can easily wed the crowd knows a feverish enjoyment which will be eternally denied to the egoist, shut up like a trunk, and to the lazy man, imprisoned like a mollusc. The poet adopts as his own all the professions, all the joys and all the miseries with which circumstance confronts him. What men call love is very meagre, very restricted and very feeble, compared to this ineffable orgy, to this holy prostitution of the soul that abandons itself entirely, poetry and charity included, to the unexpected arrival, to the passing stranger.

It is good occasionally to bring home to the happy people of this world, were it only in order to humiliate for a moment

raffinés. Les fondateurs de colonies, les pasteurs de peuples, les prêtres missionnaires exilés au bout du monde, connaissent sans doute quelque chose de ces mystérieuses ivresses; et, au sein de la vaste famille que leur génie s'est faite, ils doivent rire quelquefois de ceux qui les plaignent pour leur fortune si agitée et pour leur vie si chaste.

their inane pride, that there is a happiness superior to theirs, vaster and more refined. The founders of colonies, the pastors of peoples, missionary priests exiled to the ends of the earth, doubtless know something of this mysterious drunkenness; and, in the heart of the vast family which their genius has created for itself, they must laugh sometimes at those who pity them for their destiny that is so unquiet and for their life that is so chaste.

UN HÉMISPHÈRE DANS UNE CHEVELURE

LAISSE-MOI RESPIRER longtemps, longtemps, l'odeur de tes cheveux, y plonger tout mon visage, comme un homme altéré dans l'eau d'une source, et les agiter avec ma main comme un mouchoir odorant, pour secouer des souvenirs dans l'air.

Si tu pouvais savoir tout ce que je vois! tout ce que je sens! tout ce que j'entends dans tes cheveux! Mon âme voyage sur le parfum comme l'âme des autres hommes sur la musique.

Tes cheveux contiennent tout un rêve, plein de voilures et de mâtures, ils contiennent de grandes mers dont les moussons me portent vers de charmants climats, où l'espace est plus bleu et plus profond, où l'atmosphère est parfumée par les fruits, par les feuilles et par la peau humaine.

Dans l'océan de ta chevelure, j'entrevois un port fourmillant de chants mélancoliques, d'hommes vigoureux de toutes nations et de navires de toutes formes découpant leurs architectures fines et compliquées sur un ciel immense où se prélasse l'éternelle chaleur.

Dans les caresses de ta chevelure, je retrouve les langueurs des longues heures passées sur un divan, dans la chambre d'un beau navire, bercées par le roulis imperceptible du port, entre les pots de fleurs et les gargoulettes rafraîchissantes.

Dans l'ardent foyer de ta chevelure, je respire l'odeur du tabac mêlée à l'opium et au sucre; dans la nuit de ta chevelure, je vois resplendir l'infini de l'azur tropical; sur les rivages duvetés de ta chevelure, je m'enivre des odeurs combinées du goudron, du musc et de l'huile de coco.

Laisse-mois mordre longtemps tes tresses lourdes et noires. Quand je mordille tes cheveux élastiques et rebelles, il me semble que je mange des souvenirs.

VII

A HEMISPHERE IN A HEAD OF HAIR

❦ LONG LET me inhale, deeply, the odour of your hair, into it plunge the whole of my face, like a thirsty man into the water of a spring, and wave it in my fingers like a scented handkerchief, to shake memories into the air.

If you could know all that I see! all that I feel! all that I hear in your hair! My soul floats upon perfumes as the souls of other men upon music.

Your hair contains an entire dream, full of sails and masts; it contains vast seas whose soft monsoons bear me to delightful climates where space is deeper and bluer, where the atmosphere is perfumed with fruit, with foliage and with human skin.

In the ocean of your hair I am shown brief visions of a port resounding with melancholy songs, of vigorous men of all nations and ships of all shapes outlining their fine and complicated architectures against an immense sky where eternal heat languidly quivers.

In the caresses of your hair I recover the languor of long hours passed on a divan, in the cabin of a fine ship, rocked by the imperceptible surge of the port, between the flower-pots and the refreshing water-jugs.

In the glowing fire-grate of your hair I inhale the odour of tobacco mingled with opium and sugar; in the night of your hair I see the infinity of tropical azure resplendent; on the downed banks of your hair I inebriate myself with the mingled odours of tar, of musk and of coconut oil.

Long let me bite your heavy, black tresses. When I gnaw your elastic and rebellious hair, it seems to me that I am eating memories.

VIII

L'INVITATION AU VOYAGE

❧ IL EST un pays superbe, un pays de Cocagne, dit-on, que je rêve de visiter avec une vieille amie. Pays singulier, noyé dans les brumes de notre Nord, et qu'on pourrait appeler l'Orient de l'Occident, la Chine de l'Europe, tant la chaude et capricieuse fantaisie s'y est donné carrière, tant elle l'a patiemment et opiniâtrement illustré de ses savantes et délicates végétations.

Un vrai pays de Cocagne, où tout est beau, riche, tranquille, honnête; où le luxe a plaisir à se mirer dans l'ordre; où la vie est grasse et douce à respirer; d'où le désordre, la turbulence et l'imprévu sont exclus; où le bonheur est marié au silence; où la cuisine elle-même est poétique, grasse et excitante à la fois; où tout vous ressemble, mon cher ange.

Tu connais cette maladie fiévreuse qui s'empare de nous dans les froides misères, cette nostalgie du pays qu'on ignore, cette angoisse de la curiosité? Il est une contrée qui te ressemble, où tout est beau, riche, tranquille et honnête, où la fantaisie a bâti et décoré une Chine occidentale, où la vie est douce à respirer, où le bonheur est marié au silence. C'est là qu'il faut aller vivre, c'est là qui'il faut aller mourir!

Oui, c'est là qu'il faut aller respirer, rêver et allonger les heures par l'infini des sensations. Un musicien a écrit l'*Invitation à la valse*; quel est celui qui composera l'*Invitation au voyage*, qu'on puisse offrir à la femme aimée, à la sœur d'élection?

Oui, c'est dans cette atmosphère qu'il ferait bon vivre, — là-bas, où les heures plus lentes contiennent plus de pensées,

VIII

INVITATION TO THE VOYAGE

❧ THERE IS a majestic country, a Land of Cockaigne, they say, which I dream of visiting with an old friend; a unique country, drowned in the mists of our North, and which one might call the Orient of the Occident, the China of Europe, so greatly has fervent and capricious phantasy indulged itself there, so patiently and so obstinately has it illustrated the land with its learned and delicate vegetations.

A true Land of Cockaigne, where all is beautiful, rich, restful, decorous; where Luxury takes pleasure in seeing itself mirrored in Order; where life is heavy and sweet on the senses; whence disorder, turbulence and the unforeseen are banned; where happiness is wedded to silence; where even the fare is poetic, stimulating and rich at the same time; where all resembles you, my dear angel.

Do you know the febrile malady that possesses us in our cold wretchedness, that nostalgia for the country which we do not know, that anguish of curiosity? There is a land that resembles you, where all is beautiful, rich, restful and decorous, where phantasy has built and furnished a China of the West, where life is sweet to the senses, where happiness is wedded to silence. It is there that we must go to live, it is there that we must go to die.

Yes, this is the place where we must breathe, dream and lengthen the hours through an infinity of sensations. A musician has written the *Invitation to the Waltz*; where is he that shall compose the *Invitation to the Voyage*, which one may offer to the woman he loves, to the sister of his choice?

Yes, in this atmosphere it would be good to live, over

où les horloges sonnent le bonheur avec une plus profonde et plus significative solennité.

Sur des panneaux luisants, ou sur des cuirs dorés et d'une richesse sombre, vivent discrètement des peintures béates, calmes et profondes, comme les âmes des artistes qui les créèrent. Les soleils couchants, qui colorent si richement la salle à manger ou le salon, sont tamisés par de belles étoffes ou par ces hautes fenêtres ouvragées que le plomb divise en nombreux compartiments. Les meubles sont vastes, curieux, bizarres, armés de serrures et de secrets comme des âmes raffinées. Les miroirs, les métaux, les étoffes, l'orfèvrerie et la faïence y jouent pour les yeux une symphonie muette et mystérieuse; et de toutes choses, de tous les coins, des fissures des tiroirs et des plis des étoffes s'échappe un parfum singulier, un *revenez-y* de Sumatra, qui est comme l'âme de l'appartement.

Un vrai pays de Cocagne, te dis-je, où tout est riche, propre et luisant, comme une belle conscience, comme une magnifique batterie de cuisine, comme une splendide orfévrerie, comme une bijouterie bariolée! Les trésors du monde y affluent, comme dans la maison d'un homme laborieux et qui a bien méritéc du monde entier. Pays singulier, supérieur aux autres, comme l'Art l'est à la Nature, où celle-ci est réformée par le rêve, où elle est corrigée, embellie, refondue.

Qu'ils cherchent, qu'ils cherchent encore, qu'ils reculent sans cesse les limites de leur bonheur, ces alchimistes de l'horticulture! Qu'ils proposent des prix de soixante et de cent mille florins pour qui résoudra leurs ambitieux problèmes! Moi, j'ai trouvé ma *tulipe noire* et mon *dahlia bleu*!

Fleur incomparable, tulipe retrouvée, allégorique dahlia, c'est là, n'est-ce pas, dans ce beau pays si calme et si rêveur, qu'il faudrait aller vivre et fleurir? Ne serais-tu pas encadrée dans ton analogie, et ne pourrais-tu pas te mirer, pour parler comme les mystiques, dans ta propre *correspondance*?

Des rêves! toujours des rêves! et plus l'âme est ambitieuse et délicate, plus les rêves l'éloignent du possible. Chaque homme porte en lui sa dose d'opium naturel, incessamment sécrétée et renouvelée, et, de la naissance à la mort, combien comptons-nous d'heures remplies par la jouissance positive, par l'action réus-

there, where the slower hours contain more thoughts, where the clocks toll of happiness with a deeper and more meaningful solemnity.

On shining panels, or on leather gilt and sombrely rich, sacred paintings live discreetly, calm and profound as the souls of the artists who created them. The setting suns which give such rich colours to the dining-room or to the drawing-room are filtered through fine materials or through those high and elaborate windows which leaden bars divide into many compartments. The furniture is vast, curious, bizarre, equipped with locks and with secrets like a subtle mind. There the mirrors, the metals, the upholstery, the jewelry and the crockery play for the eyes a silent and mysterious symphony; and from all things, from all the corners, from the clefts in the chests of drawers and from the folds of the cloth materials, a peculiar perfume exudes, a *return to me*! of Sumatra, which is, as it were, the soul of the apartment.

A true Land of Cockaigne, I tell you, where all is rich, clean and shining, like a clear conscience, like a magnificent kitchen display, like a splendid piece of wrought gold, like jewels of many colours. The treasures of the world abound there, as in the house of an industrious man who has deserved well of everyone. Unique land, superior to all others, as Art is to Nature, where Nature is reformed by the dream, where it is corrected, embellished, remodelled.

Let them search, let them search still, let them incessantly defer the entry into their happiness, those alchemists of horticulture! Let them offer a prize of sixty and a hundred thousand florins to the man who shall solve their ambitious problems! As for me, I have found my *black tulip* and my *blue dahlia*.

Incomparable flower, tulip lost and found again, allegorical dahlia, it is there, is it not, in this country so calm and dreamy, that we must live and blossom? Shall you not be framed in the analogy of yourself, and can you not be mirrored, to speak like the mystics, in your own *correspondence*?

Dreams! always dreams! and the more ambitious and delicate the soul, the farther dreams remove it from what is possible. Every man carries within him his dose of natural opium,

35

sie et décidée? Vivrons-nous jamais, passerons-nous jamais dans ce tableau qu'a peint mon esprit, ce tableau qui te ressemble?

Ces trésors, ces meubles, ce luxe, cet ordre, ces parfums, ces fleurs miraculeuses, c'est toi. C'est encore toi, ces grands fleuves et ces canaux tranquilles. Ces énormes navires qu'ils charrient, tout chargés de richesses, et d'où montent les chants monotones de la manœuvre, ce sont mes pensées qui dorment ou qui roulent sur ton sein. Tu les conduis doucement vers la mer qui est l'Infini, tout en réfléchissant les profondeurs du ciel dans la limpidité de ta belle âme; — et quand, fatigués par la houle et gorgés des produits de l'Orient, ils rentrent au port natal, ce sont encore mes pensées enrichies qui reviennent de l'Infini vers toi.

incessantly secreted and renewed, and, from birth until death, how many hours can we count that are filled with positive joy, with successful and decisive action? Shall we ever live, shall we ever pass into that picture painted by my soul, the picture that resembles you?

Those treasures, that furniture, that luxury, that order, those perfumes, those miraculous flowers, they are yourself. So also are those wide rivers and those calm canals. Those enormous ships which they carry, loaded up with wealth, and from which rises the monotonous singing of the crew, these are my thoughts which sleep or which roll on your breast. You guide them softly to the ocean that is Infinity, while reflecting the depth of the sky in the limpidity of your pure soul; and when, wearied by the surge and gorged with products of the Orient, they return to their native port, these are still my thoughts, enriched, returning from the Infinite towards you.

IX

LA SOLITUDE

❧ UN GAZETIER philanthrope me dit que la solitude est mauvaise pour l'homme; et à l'appui de sa thése il cite, comme tous les incrédules, des paroles des Pères de l'Église.

Je sais que le Démon fréquente volontiers les lieux arides, et que l'Esprit de meurtre et de lubricité s'enflamme merveilleusement dans les solitudes. Mais il serait possible que cette solitude ne fût dangereuse que pour l'âme oisive et divagante qui la peuple de ses passions et de ses chimères.

Il est certain qu'un bavard, dont le suprême plaisir consiste à parler du haut d'une chaire ou d'une tribune, risquerait fort de devenir fou furieux dans l'île de Robinson. Je n'exige pas de mon gazetier les courageuses vertus de Crusoé, mais je demande qu'il ne décrète pas d'accusation les amoureux de la solitude et du mystère.

Il y a dans nos races jacassières des individus qui accepteraient avec moins de répugnance le supplice suprême, s'il leur était permis de faire du haut de l'échafaud une copieuse harangue, sans craindre que les tambours de Santerre ne leur coupassent intempestivement la parole.

Je ne les plains pas, parce que je devine que leurs effusions oratoires leur procurent des voluptés égales à celles que d'autres tirent du silence et du recueillement; mais je les méprise.

Je désire surtout que mon maudit gazetier me laisse m'amuser à ma guise. « Vous n'éprouvez donc jamais, — me dit-il, avec un ton de nez trés-apostolique, — le besoin de partager vos jouissances? » Voyez-vous le subtil envieux! Il sait que je dédaigne les siennes, et il vient s'insinuer dans les miennes, le hideux trouble-fête!

IX

SOLITUDE

❧ A PHILANTHROPIC journalist tells me that solitude is bad for mankind, and, to support his thesis, he quotes, like all unbelievers, the Fathers of the Church.

I know that willingly and often the Fiend haunts arid land, and that the Spirit of murder and of lechery flares up marvellously in deserted places. But it is not impossible that this solitude is dangerous only to the idle and wandering soul, which peoples it with its passions and its chimeras.

Undoubtedly a garrulous fellow, whose only desire is to speak from the heights of a platform or of a tribune, would run considerable risk of becoming a raving madman on Robinson's island. I do not demand of my journalist the courageous virtues of Crusoe, but I do demand that he refrain from making an accusation against the lovers of solitude and of mystery.

There are, amongst our nations of chatterboxes, individuals whose repugnance to the supreme torment would be less intense if they were permitted to harangue copiously from the heights of the scaffold, without fearing that the drums of Santerre* might unduly shorten their discourse.

I do not pity them, because I suspect that their oratorical effusions procure them delights equal to those which others derive from silence and contemplation; but I despise them.

I wish, above all, that my cursed journalist would allow me to amuse myself in my fashion. 'Can it be', he says to me with a most apostolic nasal intonation, 'that you never feel the need to share your enjoyments with others?' Just look at the subtlety of this envious fellow! He knows that I despise his joys, and he would like to insinuate himself into mine, the hideous spoil-sport!

« Ce grand malheur de ne pouvoir être seul!... » dit quelque part La Bruyère, comme pour faire honte à tous ceux qui courent s'oublier dans la foule, craignant sans doute de ne pouvoir se supporter eux-mêmes.

« Presque tous nos malheurs nous viennent de n'avoir pas su rester dans notre chambre », dit un autre sage, Pascal, je crois, rappelant ainsi dans la cellule du recueillement tous ces affolés qui cherchent le bonheur dans le mouvement et dans une prostitution que je pourrais appeler *fraternitaire*, si je voulais parler la belle langue de mon siècle.

'Oh the great misfortune of those who cannot be alone!' La Bruyère says somewhere, as though to shame all those who rush away to forget themselves in the crowd, afraid, no doubt, that they cannnot support themselves without help.

'The cause of almost all our misfortunes is our inability to sit still in our room,' says another sage, Pascal, I believe, thus recalling to the cell of contemplation all those deluded creatures who seek happiness in movement and in a prostitution which I should call *fraternistic* if I wished to speak the beautiful language of my century.

*Antoine Joseph Santerre (1752–1809), a brewer by trade, was C.-in-C. of the National Guard when Louis XVI was executed; he ordered the drummers to drown the King's voice when the latter attempted to address the crowd.

X

LES YEUX DES PAUVRES

❧ AH! VOUS voulez savoir pourquoi je vous hais aujourd'hui. Il vous sera sans doute moins facile de le comprendre qu'à moi de vous l'expliquer; car vous êtes, je crois, le plus bel exemple d'imperméabilité féminine qui se puisse rencontrer.

Nous avions passé ensemble une longue journée qui m'avait paru courte. Nous nous étions bien promis que toutes nos pensées nous seraient communes à l'un et à l'autre, et que nos deux âmes désormais n'en feraient plus qu'une; — un rêve qui n'a rien d'original, après tout, si ce n'est que, rêvé par tous les hommes, il n'a été réalisé par aucun.

Le soir, un peu fatiguée, vous voulûtes vous asseoir devant un café neuf qui formait le coin d'un boulevard neuf, encore tout plein de gravois et montrant déjà glorieusement ses splendeurs inachevées. Le café étincelait. Le gaz lui-même y déployait toute l'ardeur d'un début, et éclairait de toutes ses forces les murs aveuglants de blancheur, les nappes éblouissantes des miroirs, les ors des baguettes et des corniches, les pages aux joues rebondies traînées par les chiens en laisse, les dames riant au faucon perché sur leur poing, les nymphes et les déesses portant sur leur tête des fruits, des pâtés et du gibier, les Hébés et les Ganymèdes présentant à bras tendu la petite amphore à bavaroises ou l'obélisque bicolore des glaces panachées; toute l'histoire et toute la mythologie mises au service de la goinfrerie.

Droit devant nous, sur la chaussée, était planté un brave homme d'une quarantaine d'années, au visage fatigué, à la barbe grisonnante, tenant d'une main un petit garçon et portant sur l'autre bras un petit être trop faible pour marcher. Il remplissait l'office de bonne et faisait prendre à ses enfants

X

THE EYES OF THE POOR

❧ SO YOU would like to know why I hate you today. No doubt it will be easier for you to understand it than for me to explain it to you; for you are, I think, the finest example of feminine impermeability that one could meet.

We had spent together a long day that seemed short to me. We had promised each other that all our thoughts would be shared, and that henceforth our souls would be as one; a dream which, after all, has nothing original about it, except perhaps that, dreamed by every man, it has been fulfilled by none.

In the evening, being a little tired, you wished to sit down in front of a new café which formed the corner of a new boulevard, still full of plaster and already gloriously revealing its incomplete splendours. The café sparkled. Even the gas-light displayed all the ardour of a first appearance, and, with all its might, lit up the walls that were blindingly white, the dazzling expanse of the mirrors, the gold of the rods and the cornices, the round-cheeked page-boys pulled along by leashed dogs, the ladies smiling at falcons perched on their fingers, the nymphs and goddesses carrying fruit, pies and game on their heads, the Hebes and Ganymedes presenting with outstretched arms their little jugs decorated in the Bavarian style or their two-coloured obelisk of streaked plate-glass; the whole of history and the whole of mythology put at the service of the gormandizer's pleasure.

Straight in front of us, on the road, there stood an honest man of about forty years old, with tired features and a greying beard, who with one hand held a little boy, and on the other arm carried a little creature too feeble to walk. He was

l'air du soir. Tous en guenilles. Ces trois visages étaient extraordinairement sérieux, et ces six yeux contemplaient fixement le café nouveau avec une admiration égale, mais nuancée diversement par l'âge.

Les yeux du père disaient : « Que c'est beau! que c'est beau! on dirait que tout l'or du pauvre monde est venu se porter sur ces murs. » — Les yeux du petit garçon : « Que c'est beau! que c'est beau! mais c'est une maison où peuvent seuls entrer les gens qui ne sont pas comme nous. » — Quant aux yeux du plus petit, ils étaient trop fascinés pour exprimer autre chose qu'une joie stupide et profonde.

Les chansonniers disent que le plaisir rend l'âme bonne et amollit le cœur. La chanson avait raison ce soir-là, relativement à moi. Non-seulement j'étais attendri par cette famille d'yeux, mais je me sentais un peu honteux de nos verres et de nos carafes, plus grands que notre soif. Je tournais mes regards vers les vôtres, cher amour, pour y lire *ma* pensée; je plongeais dans vos yeux si beaux et si bizarrement doux, dans vos yeux verts, habités par le Caprice et inspirés par la Lune, quand vous me dîtes : « Ces gens-là me sont insupportables avec les yeux ouverts comme des portes cochères! Ne pourriez-vous pas prier le maître du café de les éloigner d'ici? »

Tant il est difficile de s'entendre, mon cher ange, et tant la pensée est incommunicable, même entre gens qui s'aiment!

performing the duties of nursemaid and taking his children out in the evening air. All in rags. Those three faces were extraordinarily serious, and six eyes were fixedly contemplating the new café with an admiration equally tense, though distinguished slightly by differences in age.

The father's eyes were saying : 'How beautiful it is! how beautiful it is. One would think that all the gold of the poor world has come together on these walls.' The eyes of the little boy : 'How beautiful it is! how beautiful it is! but it is a house which only people who are not like us may enter.' As for the eyes of the smallest, they were too fascinated to express anything but a stupid and profound joy.

The song-writers say that pleasure makes the soul good and softens the heart. The song was right that evening, as far as I was concerned. Not only was I moved by that family of eyes, but I felt a little ashamed of our glasses and our decanters that were larger than our thirst. I turned my eyes towards yours, my love, to read my thoughts in them; I was plunging into your eyes that are so beautiful and so strangely soft, into your green eyes inhabited by Caprice and inspired by the moon, when you said : 'Those people are unbearable, with their eyes as wide open as coach-house gates! Couldn't you ask the manager of the café to send them away?'

You see, my dear angel, how difficult it is to understand one another, and how incommunicable all thoughts are, even between people who love each other!

XI

LE JOUEUR GÉNÉREUX

❧ HIER, A travers la foule du boulevard, je me suis senti frôlé par un Etre mystérieux que j'avais toujours désiré connaître, et que je reconnus tout de suite, quoique je ne l'eusse jamais vu. Il y avait san doute chez lui, relativement à moi, un désir analogue, car il me fit, en passant, un clignement d'œil significatif auquel je me hâtai d'obéir. Je le suivis attentivement, et bientôt, je descendis derrière lui dans une demeure souterraine, éblouissante, où éclatait un luxe dont aucune des habitations supérieures de Paris ne pourrait fournir un exemple approchant. Il me parut singulier que j'eusse pu passer si souvent à côté de ce prestigieux repaire sans en deviner l'entrée. Là régnait une atmosphère exquise, quoique capiteuse, qui faisait oublier presque instantanément toutes les fastidieuses horreurs de la vie; on y respirait une béatitude sombre, analogue à celle que durent éprouver les mangeurs de lotus quand, débarquant dans une île enchantée, éclairée des lueurs d'une éternelle après-midi, ils sentirent naître en eux, aux sons assoupissants des mélodieuses cascades, le désir de ne jamais revoir leurs pénates, leurs femmes, leurs enfants, et de ne jamais remonter sur les hautes lames de la mer.

Il y avait là des visages étranges d'hommes et de femmes, marqués d'une beauté fatale, qu'il me semblait avoir vus déjà à des époques et dans des pays dont il m'était impossible de me souvenir exactement, et qui m'inspiraient plutôt une sympathie fraternelle que cette crainte qui naît ordinairement à l'aspect de l'inconnu. Si je voulais essayer de définir d'une manière quelconque l'expression singulière de leurs regards, je dirais que jamais je ne vis d'yeux brillant plus énergiquement

XI

THE GENEROUS GAMESTER

❧ YESTERDAY, IN the midst of the crowded boulevard, I felt my arm lightly touched by a mysterious Being whom I had always wanted to know, and whom I recognized at once, though I had never seen him before. No doubt he entertained a similar desire in relation to myself, for, in passing, he gave me a significant wink of the eye, which I hastened to obey. I followed him attentively, and soon I descended after him into a subterranean but dazzling abode, which shone with a luxury of which none of the finest houses of Paris could offer the shadow of an example. It seemed strange to me that I could so often have passed by the side of this prodigious haunt without divining its entrance. In that place there reigned an atmosphere both exquisite and pungent, which caused the almost instantaneous oblivion of all the exacting horrors of life; there one inhaled sombre blissfulness, similar to that which the lotus-eaters must have experienced when, disembarking on an enchanted island illumined by the glimmer of an eternal afternoon, they felt rise within them, to the narcotic sound of harmonious waterfalls, the desire never again to see their household gods, their wives, their children, and never again to ascend the high billows of the sea.

In that place there were strange faces of men and women, imprinted with a fatal beauty which, it seemed, I had already seen in epochs and in countries which I was unable to remember distinctly, and which inspired me with a kind of fraternal sympathy rather than with that fear which is usually aroused by glimpses of the unknown. If I wished to try somehow to describe the singular expression of their gaze, I should say that never have I seen eyes more energetically ablaze with

47

de l'horreur de l'ennui et du désir immortel de se sentir vivre.

Mon hôte et moi, nous étions déjà, en nous asseyant, de vieux et parfaits amis. Nous mangeâmes, nous bûmes outre mesure de toutes sortes de vins extraordinaires, et, chose non moins extraordinaire, il me semblait, après plusieurs heures, que je n'étais pas plus ivre que lui. Cependant le jeu, ce plaisir surhumain, avait coupé à divers intervalles nos fréquentes libations, et je dois dire que j'avais joué et perdu mon âme, en partie liée, avec une insouciance et une légèreté héroïques. L'âme est une chose si impalpable, si souvent inutile et quelquefois si gênante, que je n'éprouvai, quant à cette perte, qu'un peu moins d'émotion que si j'avais égaré, dans une promenade, ma carte de visite.

Nous fumâmes longuement quelques cigares dont la saveur et le parfum incomparables donnaient à l'âme la nostalgie de pays et de bonheurs inconnus, et, enivré de toutes ces délices, j'osai, dans un accès de familiarité qui ne parut pas lui déplaire, m'écrier, en m'emparant d'une coupe pleine jusqu'au bord : « A votre immortelle santé, vieux Bouc! »

Nous causâmes aussi de l'univers, de sa création et de sa future destruction; de la grande idée du siècle, c'est-à-dire du progrès et de la perfectibilité, et, en général, de toutes les formes de l'infatuation humaine. Sur ce sujet-là, Son Altesse ne tarissait pas en plaisanteries légères et irréfutables, et elle s'exprimait avec une suavité de diction et une tranquillité dans la drôlerie que je n'ai trouvées dans aucun des plus célèbres causeurs de l'humanité. Elle m'expliqua l'absurdité des différentes philosophies qui avaient jusqu'à présent pris possession du cerveau humain et daigna même me faire confidence de quelques principes fondamentaux dont il ne me convient pas de partager les bénéfices et la propriété avec qui que ce soit. Elle ne se plaignit en aucune façon de la mauvaise réputation dont elle jouit dans toutes les parties du monde, m'assura qu'elle était, elle-même, la personne la plus intéressée à la destruction de la *superstition*, et m'avoua qu'elle n'avait eu peur, relativement à son propre pouvoir, qu'une seule fois, c'était le jour où elle avait entendu un prédicateur, plus subtil que ses confrères, s'écrier en chaire : « Mes chers frères,

a horror of boredom and the immortal desire to feel conscious of being alive.

My host and myself, from the moment we took our seats, were perfect friends. We ate, we drank immoderately all sorts of extraordinary wines, and, a circumstance not less extraordinary, it seemed to me, after several hours, that I was not more drunk than he. However, gambling, that superhuman amusement, had interrupted our libations at frequent intervals, and I must say that in partnership I had staked and lost my soul with heroic indifference and frivolity. The soul is a thing so impalpable, so often useless, and sometimes so embarrassing that at this loss I felt only a little more emotion than if, during a walk, I had lost my visiting card.

For a long time we smoked some cigars whose incomparable savour and scent filled the soul with the longing for unknown countries and unknown joys, and, drunk with all these delights, in a fit of familiarity which did not seem to displease him, I had the courage to cry out, while taking hold of a cup filled to the brim : 'To your immortal health, old Satyr!'

We spoke also of the universe, of its creation and of its future destruction; of the great idea of the century, that is to say of progress and perfectibility, and generally all the forms of human infatuation. On this subject His Highness lavished an inexhaustible fund of subtle and irrefutable witticisms, and he expressed himself with a suavity of diction and dryness of wit which I have not found in any of the most famous conversationalists of humanity. He explained to me the absurdity of the different philosophies which had, up to the present time, taken possession of the human brain, and even condescended to confide to me some fundamental principles, the benefits and propriety of which I may not befittingly share with anyone at all. He did not complain in any way of the bad reputation which he enjoys in all parts of the world, assured me that he was himself the person most interested in the destruction of *superstition*, and confessed to me that only on one occasion had he feared for his own power, that is, the day on which he had heard a preacher more subtle than his fellows call out from

n'oubliez jamais, quand vous entendrez vanter le progrès des lumières, que la plus belle des ruses du diable est de vous persuader qu'il n'existe pas! »

Le souvenir de ce célèbre orateur nous conduisit naturellement vers le sujet des académies, et mon étrange convive m'affirma qu'il ne dédaignait pas, en beaucoup de cas, d'inspirer la plume, la parole et la conscience des pédagogues, et qu'il assistait presque toujours en personne, quoique invisible, à toutes les séances académiques.

Encouragé par tant de bontés, je lui demandai des nouvelles de Dieu, et s'il l'avait vu récemment. Il me répondit, avec une insouciance nuancée d'une certaine tristesse : « Nous nous saluons quand nous nous rencontrons, mais comme deux vieux gentilshommes, en qui une politesse innée ne saurait éteindre tout à fait le souvenir d'anciennes rancunes. »

Il est douteux que Son Altesse ait jamais donné une si longue audience à un simple mortel, et je craignais d'abuser. Enfin, comme l'aube frissonnante blanchissait les vitres, ce célèbre personnage, chanté par tant de poëtes et servi par tant de philosophes qui travaillent à sa gloire sans le savoir, me dit : « Je veux que vous gardiez de moi un bon souvenir, et vous prouver que Moi, dont on dit tant de mal, je suis quelquefois *bon diable*, pour me servir d'une de vos locutions vulgaires. Afin de compenser la perte irrémédiable que vous avez faite de votre âme, je vous donne l'enjeu que vous auriez gagné si le sort avait été pour vous, c'est-à-dire la possibilité de soulager et de vaincre, pendant toute votre vie, cette bizarre affection de l'Ennui, qui est la source de toutes vos maladies et de tous vos misérables progrès. Jamais un désir ne sera formé par vous, que je ne vous aide à le réaliser; vous régnerez sur vos vulgaires semblables; vous serez fourni de flatteries et même d'adorations; l'argent, l'or, les diamants, les palais féeriques, viendront vous chercher et vous prieront de les accepter, sans que vous ayez fait un effort pour les gagner; vous changerez de patrie et de contrée aussi souvent que votre fantaisie vous l'ordonnera; vous vous soûlerez de voluptés, sans lassitude, dans des pays charmants où il fait toujours

the pulpit : 'My dear brethren, never forget, when you hear boasts about the progress of enlightenment, that the finest ruse of the devil is to persuade you that he does not exist.!'

The memory of this famous orator led us naturally towards the subject of the academies, and my strange companion assured me that in many cases he did not disdain to inspire the pen, the spoken word and the conscience of pedagogues, and that he almost invariably attended every session of the academies in person, though invisible.

Encouraged by so many kindnesses, I asked him news of God, and whether he had seen Him recently. With a carefree air tinted with a certain sadness he replied : 'We raise our hats to each other when we meet, but like two old noblemen, in whom an innate politeness cannot quite extinguish the memory of former grievances.'

It is doubtful whether His Highness has ever given such a long audience to a simple mortal, and I was afraid of abusing his condescension. At last, when shuddering dawn whitened the window-panes, this famous personage, sung by so many poets and served by so many philosophers who work for his glory without knowing it, said to me : 'I should like you to preserve a happy memory of me, and to prove to you that I, of whom so much evil is spoken, am sometimes a *kind old devil*, to use one of your vulgar phrases. In order to compensate you for the irrecoverable loss which you have sustained, that of your soul, I give you the prize that you would have won if fate had been on your side, that is to say, the possibility of relieving and and overcoming, all your life long, that strange affliction of Boredom, which is the source of all your disorders and of all your miserable progress. Never shall a desire be formed by you which I shall not help you to realize; you shall reign over your vulgar fellows; you shall be provided with flattery and even with adoration; silver, gold and diamonds, fairy palaces shall go in search of you and shall implore you to accept them, without your having made an effort to earn them; you shall have a change of country and of scenery as often as your fancy commands it; you shall ine-

chaud et où les femmes sentent aussi bon que les fleurs, — et cætera, et cætera . . . », ajouta-t-il en se levant et en me congédiant avec un bon sourire.

Si ce n'eût été la crainte de l'humilier devant une aussi grande assemblée, je serais volontiers tombé aux pieds de ce joueur généreux pour le remercier de son inouïe munificence. Mais peu à peu, après que je l'eus quitté, l'incurable défiance rentra dans mon sein; je n'osais plus croire à un si prodigieux bonheur, et, en me couchant, faisant encore ma prière par un reste d'habitude imbécile, je répétais dans un demi-sommeil : « Mon Dieu! Seigneur, mon Dieu! faites que le diable me tienne sa parole! »

briate yourself with sensual delights, without weariness, in those enchanting countries where it is always warm and where the women smell like flowers. Et cetera . . .' he added, rising, and dismissing me with a gracious smile.

Had it not been for the fear of humiliating myself before such a large assembly, I would gladly have fallen at the feet of this generous gamester, to thank him for his unprecedented open-handedness. But after I had left him, little by little, that incurable distrust of mine entered once more into my heart; I dared no longer believe in such a prodigious happiness, and when, before going to bed, compelled by the residue of an idiotic habit, I again said my prayers, I drowsily muttered again and again : 'O God! O Lord God! Make the devil keep his promise!'

XII

ENIVREZ-VOUS

IL FAUT être toujours ivre. Tout est là : c'est l'unique question. Pour ne pas sentir l'horrible fardeau du Temps qui brise vos épaules et vous penche vers la terre, il faut vous enivrer sans trêve.

Mais de quoi? De vin, de poésie ou de vertu, à votre guise. Mais enivrez-vous.

Et si quelquefois, sur les marches d'un palais, sur l'herbe verte d'un fossé, dans la solitude morne de votre chambre, vous vous réveillez, l'ivresse déjà diminuée ou disparue, demandez au vent, à la vague, à l'étoile, à l'oiseau, à l'horloge, à tout ce qui fuit, à tout ce qui gémit, à tout ce qui roule, à tout ce qui chante, à tout ce qui parle, demandez quelle heure il est; et le vent, la vague, l'étoile, l'oiseau, l'horloge, vous répondront : « Il est l'heure de s'enivrer! Pour n'être pas les esclaves martyrisés du Temps, enivrez-vous; enivrez-vous sans cesse! De vin, de poésie ou de vertu, à votre guise. »

XII

GET DRUNK!

❧ ONE SHOULD always be drunk. That's all that matters; that's our one imperative need. So as not to feel Time's horrible burden that breaks your shoulders and bows you down, you must get drunk without ceasing.

But what with? With wine, with poetry, or with virtue, as you choose. But get drunk.

And if, at some time, on the steps of a palace, in the green grass of a ditch, in the bleak solitude of your room, you are waking up when drunkenness has already abated, ask the wind, the wave, a star, the clock, all that which flees, all that which groans, all that which rolls, all that which sings, all that which speaks, ask them what time it is; and the wind, the wave, the star, the bird, the clock will reply : 'It is time to get drunk! So that you may not be the martyred slaves of Time, get drunk; get drunk, and never pause for rest! With wine, with poetry, or with virtue, as you choose!'

XIII

LES BIENFAITS DE LA LUNE

LA LUNE, qui est le caprice même, regarda par la fenêtre pendant que tu dormais dans ton berceau, et se dit : « Cette enfant me plaît. »

Et elle descendit moelleusement son escalier de nuages, et passa sans bruit à travers les vitres. Puis elle s'étendit sur toi avec la tendresse souple d'une mère, et elle déposa ses couleurs sur ta face. Tes prunelles en sont restées vertes, et tes joues extraordinairement pâles. C'est en contemplant cette visiteuse que tes yeux se sont si bizarrement agrandis; et elle t'a si tendrement serrée à la gorge que tu en as gardé pour toujours l'envie de pleurer.

Cependant, dans l'expansion de sa joie, la Lune remplissait toute la chambre, comme une atmosphère phosphorique, comme un poison lumineux; et toute cette lumière vivante pensait et disait : « Tu subiras éternellement l'influence de mon baiser. Tu seras belle à ma manière. Tu aimeras ce que j'aime et ce qui m'aime : l'eau, les nuages, le silence et la nuit; la mer immense et verte; l'eau informe et multiforme; le lieu où tu ne seras pas; l'amant que tu ne connaîtras pas; les fleurs monstrueuses; les parfums qui font délirer; les chats qui se pâment sur les pianos et qui gémissent comme les femmes, d'une voix rauque et douce!

« Et tu seras aimée de mes amants, courtisée par mes courtisans. Tu seras la reine des hommes aux yeux verts dont j'ai serré aussi la gorge dans mes caresses nocturnes; de ceux-là qui aiment la mer, la mer immense, tumultueuse et verte, l'eau informe et multiforme, le lieu où ils ne sont pas, la femme qu'ils ne connaissent pas, les fleurs sinistres qui res-

XIII

THE FAVOURS OF THE MOON

❧ THE MOON, who is caprice itself, looked through the window while you were sleeping in your cradle, and said to herself : 'I like this child.'

And softly she descended her staircase of clouds and, noiselessly, passed through the window-panes. Then she stretched herself out over you with the supple tenderness of a mother, and laid down her colours on your face. Ever since, the pupils of your eyes have remained green and your cheeks unusually pale. It was while contemplating this visitor that your eyes became so strangely enlarged; and she clasped your neck so tenderly that you have retained for ever the desire to weep.

However, in the expansion of her joy, the Moon filled the whole room like a phosphorescent vapour, like a luminous poison; and all the living light thought and said : 'You shall suffer for ever the influence of my kiss. You shall be beautiful in my fashion. You shall love that which I love and that which loves me : water, clouds, silence and the night; the immense green sea; the formless and multiform streams; the place where you shall not be; the lover whom you shall not know; flowers of monstrous shape; perfumes that cause delirium; cats that shudder, swoon and curl up on pianos and groan like women, with a voice that is hoarse and gentle!

'And you shall be loved by my lovers, courted by my courtiers. You shall be the queen of all men that have green eyes, whose necks also I have clasped in my noctural caresses; of those who love the sea, the sea that is immense, tumultuous and green, the formless and multiform streams, the place where they are not, the woman whom they do not know,

semblent aux encensoirs d'une religion inconnue, les parfums qui troublent la volonté, et les animaux sauvages et voluptueux qui sont les emblèmes de leur folie. »

Et c'est pour cela, maudite chère enfant gâtée, que je suis maintenant couché à tes pieds, cherchant dans toute ta personne le reflet de la redoutable Divinité, de la fatidique marraine, de la nourrice empoisonneuse de tous les *lunatiques*.

sinister flowers that resemble the censers of a strange religion, perfumes that confound the will; and the savage and voluptuous animals which are the emblems of their dementia.'

And that, my dear, cursed, spoiled child, is why I am now lying at your feet, seeking in all your person the reflection of the formidable divinity, of the foreknowing godmother, the poisoning wet-nurse of all the *lunatics*.

XIV

LAQUELLE EST LA VRAIE?

❦ J'AI CONNU une certaine Bénédicta, qui remplissait l'atmosphère d'idéal, et dont les yeux répandaient le désir de la grandeur, de la beauté, de la gloire et de tout ce qui fait croire à l'immortalité.

Mais cette fille miraculeuse était trop belle pour vivre long-temps; aussi est-elle morte quelques jour après que j'eus fait sa connaissance, et c'est moi-même qui l'ai enterrée, un jour que le printemps agitait son encensoir jusque dans les cimetières. C'est moi qui l'ai enterrée, bien close dans une bière d'un bois parfumé et incorruptible comme les coffres de l'Inde.

Et comme mes yeux restaient fichés sur le lieu où était enfoui mon trésor, je vis subitement une petite personne qui ressemblait singulièrement à le défunte, et qui, piétinant sur la terre fraîche avec une violence hystérique et bizarre, disait en éclatant de rire : « C'est moi, la vraie Bénédicta! C'est moi, une fameuse canaille! Et pour la punition de ta folie et de ton aveuglement, tu m'aimeras telle que je suis! «

Mais moi, furieux, j'ai répondu : « Non! non! non! » Et pour mieux accentuer mon refus, j'ai frappé si violemment la terre du pied que ma jambe s'est enfoncée jusqu'au genou dans la sépulture récente, et que, comme un loup pris au piége, je reste attaché, pour toujours peut-être, à la fosse de l'idéal.

XIV

WHICH IS THE TRUE ONE?

❧ I ONCE knew a certain Benedicta, who filled the atmosphere with emanations of the ideal, and whose eyes inspired others with the desire for greatness, for beauty, for glory and for all those qualities that make us believe in immortality.

But this miraculous girl was too beautiful to live long; indeed she died a few days after I made her acquaintance, and it was I who buried her one day when the spring was swinging its censer even into the cemeteries. It was I who buried her, well sealed in a coffin made of a wood perfumed and incorruptible as the coffers of India.

And as my eyes remained fixed upon the place where my treasure lay hidden, suddenly I saw a little person who bore a singular resemblance to her who was dead, and who, trampling upon the fresh soil with hysterical and fantastical violence, said, amidst a peal of loud laughter : 'It is I, the true Benedicta! It is I, a fine, worthless wretch! and as a punishment for your infatuation and for your self-delusion, you shall love me as I am.'

But, furious, I replied : 'No! No! No!' And, to add emphasis to my refusal, I struck the ground so violently with my foot that my leg sank knee-deep into the fresh soil, and like a wolf caught in a trap, I remain attached, for ever perhaps, to the grave of the ideal.

XV

LE MIROIR

UN HOMME épouvantable entre et se regarde dans la glace.

« — Pourquoi vous regardez-vous au miroir, puisque vous ne pouvez vous y voir qu'avec déplaisir? »

L'homme épouvantable me répond : « — Monsieur, d'après les immortels principes de 89, tous les hommes sont égaux en droits; donc je possède le droit de me mirer; avec plaisir ou déplaisir, cela ne regarde que ma conscience. »

Au nom du bon sens, j'avais sans doute raison; mais, au point de vue de la loi, il n'avait pas tort.

XV

THE MIRROR

❧ A MAN of horrifying aspect enters the room and looks at himself in the glass.

"Why are you looking at yourself in the mirror, since you cannot see your reflection without displeasure?"

The man of horrifying aspect replies to my question:

'Sir, according to the immortal principles of the '89 Revolution, all men have equal rights; therefore I possess the right to look at myself in the mirror; whether with pleasure or with displeasure, that concerns only my conscience.'

As a spokesman for good sense, I was undoubtedly right; but from the point of view of the law, he was not wrong.

XVI

LE PORT

❧ UN PORT est un séjour charmant pour une âme fatiguée des luttes de la vie. L'ampleur du ciel, l'architecture mobile des nuages, les colorations changeantes de la mer, le scintillement des phares, sont un prisme merveilleusement propre à amuser les yeux sans jamais les lasser. Les formes élancées des navires, au gréement compliqué, auxquels la houle imprime des oscillations harmonieuses, servent à entretenir dans l'âme le goût du rythme et de la beauté. Et puis, surtout, il y a une sorte de plaisir mystérieux et aristocratique pour celui qui n'a plus ni curiosité ni ambition, à contempler, couché dans le belvédère ou accoudé sur le môle, tous ces mouvements de ceux qui partent et de ceux qui reviennent, de ceux qui ont encore la force de vouloir, le désir de voyager ou de s'enrichir.

XVI

THE PORT

❧ A PORT is a delightful place of rest for a soul weary of life's battles. The vastness of the sky, the mobile architecture of the clouds, the changing colouration of the sea, the twinkling of the lights, are a prism marvellously fit to amuse the eyes without ever tiring them. The slender shapes of the ships with their complicated rigging, to which the surge lends harmonious oscillations, serve to sustain within the soul the taste for rhythm and beauty. Also, and above all, for the man who no longer possesses either curiosity or ambition, there is a kind of mysterious and aristocratic pleasure in contemplating, while lying on the belvedere or resting his elbows on the jetty-head, all these movements of men who are leaving and men who are returning, of those who still have the strength to will, the desire to travel or to enrich themselves.

XVII

LA SOUPE ET LES NUAGES

MA PETITE folle bien-aimée me donnait à dîner, et par la fenêtre ouverte de la salle à manger je contemplais les mouvantes architectures que Dieu fait avec les vapeurs, les merveilleuses constructions de l'impalpable. Et je me disais, à travers ma contemplation : « — Toutes ces fantasmagories sont presque aussi belles que vastes les yeux de ma belle bien-aimée, la petite folle monstrueuse aux yeux verts. »

Et tout à coup je reçus un violent coup de poing dans le dos, et j'entendis une voix rauque et charmante, une voix hystérique et comme enrouée par l'eau-de-vie, la voix de ma chère petite bien-aimée, qui disait : « — Allez-vous bientôt manger votre soupe, sacré bougre de marchand de nuages? »

XVII

THE SOUP AND THE CLOUDS

❧ MY LITTLE mad darling was giving me my dinner, and through the open window of the dining-room I was contemplating the moving architectures that God makes out of vapours, those marvellous constructions of the impalpable. And I said to myself, in the midst of my meditation : 'All those phantasmagoria are almost as beautiful as the eyes of my beloved, that monstrous little mad woman with the green eyes.'

And suddenly I received a violent blow on my back, and I heard a charming, raucous voice, a voice hysterical and as though made hoarse by brandy, the voice of my sweet little darling who was saying : 'Well, are you going to eat your soup or aren't you, you bloody dithering cloud-monger?'

XVIII

PERTE D'AURÉOLE

« EH! QUOI! vous ici, mon cher? Vous, dans un mauvais lieu! vous, le buveur de quintessences! vous, le mangeur d'ambroisie! En vérité, il y a là de quoi me surprendre.

— Mon cher, vous connaissez ma terreur des chevaux et des voitures. Tout à l'heure, comme je traversais le boulevard, en grande hâte, et que je sautillais dans la boue, à travers ce chaos mouvant où la mort arrive au galop de tous les côtés à la fois, mon auréole, dans un mouvement brusque, a glissé de ma tête dans la fange du macadam. Je n'ai pas eu le courage de la ramasser. J'ai jugé moins désagréable de perdre mes insignes que de me faire rompre les os. Et puis, me suis-je dit, à quelque chose malheur est bon. Je puis maintenant me promener incognito, faire des actions basses, et me livrer à la crapule, comme les simple mortels. Et me voici, tout semblable à vous, comme vous voyez!

— Vous devriez au moins faire afficher cette auréole, ou la faire réclamer par le commissaire.

— Ma foi! non. Je me trouve bien ici. Vous seul, vous m'avez reconnu. D'ailleurs la dignité m'ennuie. Ensuite je pense avec joie que quelque mauvais poëte la ramassera et s'en coiffera impudemment. Faire un heureux, quelle jouissance! et surtout un heureux qui me fera rire! Pensez à X, ou à Z! Hein! comme ce sera drôle! »

XVIII

LOSS OF A HALO

❧ 'WHAT! YOU here, my dear fellow? You, in an evil place? You, the drinker of quintessences, the eater of ambrosia! To be sure, I am surprised at you.'

'My dear friend, you know my terror of horses and carriages. Not long ago, as I was crossing the boulevard in great haste, and as I was hopping about in the mud, through this shifting chaos where death arrives at a gallop from every direction, my halo slipped from my head during a sudden movement and fell into the mire on the macadam road. I didn't have the courage to pick it up. I thought it less disagreeable to lose my insignia than to have my bones broken. And besides, I said to myself, no misfortune is without its consolations. From now on I shall be able to walk about incognito, commit low actions, abandon myself to debauchery like ordinary mortals. And so here I am, a man just like yourself, as you can see!'

'You should at least have a notice put up about your halo, or ask the commissioner to retrieve it.'

'My goodness, no. I am quite happy as I am. You alone have recognized me. Besides, dignity bores me. Also it gives me pleasure to think that some bad poet may pick it up and impudently place it on his head. What a joy, to give happiness to a man! And, what's more, to give happiness to a man who'll make me laugh. Think of X, or of Z! What a joke that would be!'

XIX

ANY WHERE OUT OF THE WORLD
N'IMPORTE OÙ HORS DU MONDE

❧ CETTE VIE est un hôpital où chaque malade est possédé du désir de changer de lit. Celui-ci voudrait souffrir en face du poêle, et celui-là croit qu'il guérirait à côté de la fenêtre.

Il me semble que je serais toujours bien là où je ne suis pas, et cette question de déménagement en est une que je discute sans cesse avec mon âme.

« Dis-moi, mon âme, pauvre âme refroidie, que penserais-tu d'habiter Lisbonne? Il doit y faire chaud, et tu t'y ragaillardirais comme un lézard. Cette ville est au bord de l'eau; on dit qu'elle est bâtie en marbre, et que le peuple y a une telle haine du végétal, qu'il arrache tous les arbres. Voilà un paysage selon ton goût; un paysage fait avec la lumière et le minéral, et le liquide pour les réfléchir! »

Mon âme ne répond pas.

« Puisque tu aimes tant le repos, avec le spectacle du mouvement, veux-tu venir habiter la Hollande, cette terre béatifiante? Peut-être te divertiras-tu dans cette contrée dont tu as souvent admiré l'image dans les musées. Que penserais-tu de Rotterdam, toi qui aimes les forêts de mâts, et les navires amarrés au pied des maisons? »

Mon âme reste muette.

« Batavia te sourirait peut-être davantage? Nous y trouverions d'ailleurs l'esprit de l'Europe marié à la beauté tropicale. »

Pas un mot. — Mon âme serait-elle morte?

« En es-tu donc venue à ce point d'engourdissement que tu ne te plaises que dans ton mal? S'il en est ainsi, fuyons vers les

XIX

ANYWHERE OUT OF THE WORLD*

❧ THIS LIFE is a hospital where every patient is possessed with the desire to change beds; one man would like to suffer in front of the stove, and another believes that he would recover his health beside the window.

It always seems to me that I should feel well in the place where I am not, and this question of removal is one which I discuss incessantly with my soul.

'Tell me, my soul, poor chilled soul, what do you think of going to live in Lisbon? It must be warm there, and there you would invigorate yourself like a lizard. This city is on the sea-shore; they say that it is built of marble and that the people there have such a hatred of vegetation that they uproot all the trees. There you have a landscape that corresponds to your taste! a landscape made of light and mineral, and liquid to reflect them!

My soul does not reply.

'Since you are so fond of stillness, coupled with the show of movement, would you like to settle in Holland, that beatifying country? Perhaps you would find some diversion in that land whose image you have so often admired in the art galleries. What do you think of Rotterdam, you who love forests of masts, and ships moored at the foot of houses?'

My soul remains silent.

'Perhaps Batavia attracts you more? There we should find, amongst other things, the spirit of Europe married to tropical beauty.'

Not a word. Could my soul be dead?

'Is it then that you have reached such a degree of lethargy that you acquiesce in your sickness? If so, let us flee to lands

pays qui sont les analogies de la Mort. — Je tiens notre affaire, pauvre âme! Nous ferons nos malles pour Tornéa. Allons plus loin encore, à l'extrême bout de la Baltique; encore plus loin de la vie, si c'est possible; installons-nous au pôle. Là le soleil ne frise qu'obliquement la terre, et les lentes alternatives de la lumière et de la nuit suppriment la variété et augmentent la monotonie, cette moitié du néant. Là, nous pourrons prendre de longs bains de ténèbres, cependant que, pour nous divertir, les aurores boréales nous enverront de temps en temps leurs gerbes roses, comme des reflets d'un feu d'artifice de l'Enfer! »

Enfin, mon âme fait explosion, et sagement elle me crie : « N'importe où! n'importe où! pourvu que ce soit hors de ce monde! »

that are analogues of death. I see how it is, poor soul! We shall pack our trunks for Tornio. Let us go farther still to the extreme end of the Baltic; or farther still from life, if that is possible; let us settle at the Pole. There the sun only grazes the earth obliquely, and the slow alternation of light and darkness suppresses variety and increases monotony, that half-nothingness. There we shall be able to take long baths of darkness, while for our amusement the aurora borealis shall send us its rose-coloured rays that are like the reflection of Hell's own fireworks!'

At last my soul explodes, and wisely cries out to me : 'No matter where! No matter where! As long as it's out of the world!'

* The title of the original is in English; it is a quotation from Thomas Hood's 'The Bridge of Sighs.'

XX

ASSOMMONS LES PAUVRES!

❦ PENDANT QUINZE jours je m'étais confiné dans ma chambre, et je m'étais entouré des livres à la mode dans ce temps-là (il y a seize ou dix-sept ans); je veux parler des livres où il est traité de l'art de rendre les peuples heureux, sages et riches, en vingt-quatre heures. J'avais donc digéré, — avalé, veux-je dire, — toutes les élucubrations de tous ces entrepreneurs de bonheur public, — de ceux qui conseillent à tous les pauvres de se faire esclaves, et de ceux qui leur persuadent qu'ils sont tous des rois détrônés. — On ne trouvera pas surprenant que je fusse alors dans un état d'esprit avoisinant le vertige ou la stupidité.

Il m'avait semblé seulement que je sentais, confiné au fond de mon intellect, le germe obscur d'une idée supérieure à toutes les formules de bonne femme dont j'avais récemment parcouru le dictionnaire. Mais ce n'était que l'idée d'une idée, quelque chose d'infiniment vague.

Et je sortis avec une grande soif. Car le goût passionné des mauvaises lectures engendre un besoin proportionnel du grand air et des rafraîchissants.

Comme j'allais entrer dans un cabaret, un mendiant me tendit son chapeau, avec un de ces regards inoubliables qui culbuteraient les trônes, si l'esprit remuait la matière, et si l'œil d'un magnétiseur faisait mûrir les raisins.

En même temps, j'entendis une voix qui chuchotait à mon oreille, une voix que je reconnus bien; c'était celle d'un bon Ange, ou d'un bon Démon, qui m'accompagne partout. Puisque Socrate avait son bon Démon, pourquoi n'aurais-je pas mon bon Ange, et pourquoi n'aurais-je pas l'honneur, comme Socrate, d'obtenir mon brevet de folie, signé du subtil

XX

LET'S BEAT UP THE POOR

❧ FOR A fortnight I had confined myself to my room, and had surrounded myself with books in fashion at that time (sixteen or seventeen years ago)*; I am speaking of those books which deal with the art of making the people happy, wise and rich, in twenty-four hours. I had therefore digested — swallowed whole, I should say — all the elucubrations of all the contractors of the public weal, of those who advise all the poor people to become slaves, and of those who persuade them that they are all dethroned kings. You will not be surprised, therefore, that I was in a state of mind approaching giddiness or stupefaction.

Only it seemed to me that I felt, hidden in the depths of my mind, the obscure germ of an idea superior to all those old women's formulae, the dictionary of which I had recently perused. But this was no more than the idea of an idea, something infinitely vague.

And I went out feeling very thirsty. For the impassioned delight in bad literature engenders a corresponding need of the open air and of refreshments.

When I was about to enter a wine-shop, a beggar held out his cap to me with one of those unforgettable looks which would demolish thrones, if spirit could move matter and if the eye of a mesmerist could ripen grapes.

At the same time I heard a voice that whispered into my ear, a voice that I recognized easily; it was that of a good Angel, or a good Demon, who accompanies me everywhere. Since Socrates had his good Demon, why should not I have my good Angel, and why should not I have the honour, like Socrates, of obtaining my certificate of insanity, signed by the

Lélut et du bien-avisé Baillarger?

Il existe cette différence entre le Démon de Socrate et le mien, que celui de Socrate ne se manifestait à lui que pour défendre, avertir, empêcher, et que le mien daigne conseiller, suggérer, persuader. Ce pauvre Socrate n'avait qu'un Démon prohibiteur; le mien est un grand affirmateur, le mien est un Démon d'action, ou Démon de combat.

Or, sa voix me chuchotait ceci : « Celui-là seul est l'égal d'un autre, qui le prouve, et celui-là seul est digne de la liberté, qui sait la conquérir. »

Immédiatement, je sautai sur mon mendiant. D'un seul coup de poing, je lui bouchai un œil, qui devint, en une seconde, gros comme une balle. Je cassai un de mes ongles à lui briser deux dents, et comme je ne me sentais pas assez fort, étant né délicat et m'étant peu exercé à la boxe, pour assommer rapidement ce vieillard, je le saisis d'une main par le collet de son habit, de l'autre, je l'empoignai à la gorge, et je me mis à lui secouer vigoureusement la tête contre un mur. Je dois avouer que j'avais préalablement inspecté les environs d'un coup d'œil, et que j'avais vérifié que dans cette banlieue déserte, je me trouvais, pour un assez long temps, hors de la portée de tout agent de police.

Ayant ensuite, par un coup de pied lancé dans le dos, assez énergique pour briser les omoplates, terrassé ce sexagénaire affaibli, je me saisis d'une grosse branche d'arbre qui traînait à terre, et je le battis avec l'énergie obstinée des cuisiniers qui veulent attendrir un beefsteak.

Tout à coup, — ô miracle! ô jouissance du philosophe qui vérifie l'excellence de sa théorie! — je vis cette antique carcasse se retourner, se redresser avec une énergie que je n'aurais jamais soupçonnée dans une machine si singulièrement détraquée, et, avec un regard de haine qui me parut de *bon augure*, le malandrin décrépit se jeta sur moi, me pocha les deux yeux, me cassa quatre dents, et, avec la même branche d'arbre, me battit dru comme plâtre. — Par mon énergique médication, je lui avais donc rendu l'orgueil et la vie.

Alors, je lui fis force signes pour lui faire comprendre que je considérais le discussion comme finie, et me relevant avec la

subtle Lélut* and the prudent Baillarger?**

There is this difference between the Demon of Socrates and my own : that of Socrates only manifested himself to him in order to forbid, to warn, to prevent, while mine deigns to advise, to suggest, to persuade. Poor Socrates only had a prohibiting Demon; mine is a great affirmer, mine is a Demon of action, a Demon of combat.

Well, his voice whispered the following words : 'Only he is the equal of another who proves it, and only he is worthy of liberty who can conquer it.'

Immediately I threw myself at my beggar. With a single blow of the fist I closed one of his eyes, which, within a second, became as large as a tennis-ball. I cracked one of my finger-nails in breaking two of his teeth, and, since (being congenitally delicate and having little experience of boxing) I did not feel strong enough rapidly to knock down this old man, I seized him by the collar of his suit with one hand, clutched his throat with the other, and began vigorously to knock his head against a wall. I must confess that I had previously inspected the surroundings with one quick glance and ascertained that in this deserted suburb I should be, for a sufficiently long time, beyond the reach of all policemen.

Having then, by a kick aimed at the back with sufficient force to break the shoulder-blades, felled this enfeebled sexagenarian, I took hold of a large and low-hanging branch of a tree and beat him with the obstinate energy of cooks who wish to soften a beefsteak.

Suddenly — O miracle! O rejoicing of the philosopher who has verified the excellence of his theory — I saw this antique carcass turn round, straighten himself with an energy that I should never have suspected in a machine so singularly disordered, and with a look of hatred which I considered a *good omen*, the decrepit ruffian hurled himself upon me, blackened both my eyes, broke four of my teeth, and with the same branch of the tree, beat me soft as plaster. By my energetic medical aid, then, I had given back to him both pride and life.

Then I made many signs to the effect that I considered the discussion at an end, and getting up with the satisfaction of a

satisfaction d'un sophiste du Portique, je lui dis : « Monsieur, *vous êtes mon égal!* veuillez me faire l'honneur de partager avec moi ma bourse; et souvenez-vous, si vous êtes réellement philanthrope, qu'il faut appliquer à tous vos confrères, quand ils vous demanderont l'aumône, la théorie que j'ai eu la *douleur* d'essayer sur votre dos. »

Il m'a bien juré qu'il avait compris ma théorie, et qu'il obéirait à mes conseils.

sophist of the Portico, I said to him : 'Sir, *you are my equal*, be kind enough to do me the honor of sharing my purse with me; and remember that if you are truly philanthropic, you must apply to all your colleagues, when they ask you for alms, the theory which I have had the *anguish* of trying out on your back.'

And, sure enough, he protested that he had understood my theory and would take my advice.

* About 1850 — Translator.

* Dr Lélut, a well-known psychiatrist of his day, wrote a treatise, *Du Démon de Socrate*, in which the 'genius' of Socrates is explained away psychologically. Baudelaire himself was to suffer the same fate posthumously at the hands of Dr René Laforgue; and it is interesting to know his own opinion of such psychic dissection (see Laforgue, *L'Échec de Baudelaire*).

** Dr Baillarger (1806-91) was employed at the lunatic asylum of Ivry and later at the Salpêtrière. He lectured and wrote books about mental diseases, one of which, *Essai de classification des maladies mentales* (1854) was, for a long time, used as an authoritative textbook.

SELECTED BIBLIOGRAPHY

A list of the principal works of Charles Baudelaire,
with the dates of their first appearance

LES FLEURS DU MAL
(Paris, 1857; second augmented edition, Paris, 1861)

LES PARADIS ARTIFICIELS
(Paris, 1860)

L'ART ROMANTIQUE
(Paris, 1868)

PETITS POÈMES EN PROSE
(Paris, 1869)

ŒVRES COMPLÈTES, ed. Jacques Crépet. Includes the
correspondence
(Paris, 1922-53)

ŒVRES COMPLÈTES, ed. Le Dantec. 2 vols., including
the translations from Poe, but not the correspondence
(Editions de la Pléiade, Paris, 1944)

THE AUTHOR

Charles Baudelaire was born in Paris on April 9th, 1821. His father, born in 1759, died when Charles was six years old. His mother remarried in 1828. His relationship with his stepfather, Captain (and finally General) Aupick, was a difficult one, especially in later years. Baudelaire was sent to a boarding school in Lyons, then attended the Lycée Louis-le-Grande in Paris. He began to write poems while at school. In 1839 he was expelled from the Lycée, and became a boarder once more at a crammer's, passing his *baccalauréat* in 1839. He spent the next few years living as a bohemian in the Latin Quarter. In June 1841 he set out on a voyage to the East, an experience that left many traces in his later poems. After his return to France in 1842 he settled in Paris once more, living on his inheritance. He was notorious at this time as a dandy and drug addict. Soon he was in serious financial difficulties, which increased with the years, since Baudelaire would never accept employment of any kind, and his literary output was small. His early association with the mulatto actress Jeanne Duval continued throughout his life, at least sporadically. Baudelaire's notoriety after the publication and persecution of his *Les Fleurs du Mal* in 1857 did not relieve the poverty and loneliness of his later years. After an unsuccessful lecture tour in Belgium he became seriously ill in 1865 with general paralysis, and died in August 1867. His great international reputation, mainly as a poet but also as a literary and art critic, was mainly posthumous.